Roger Hudson
Solo Guitar Works Volume 2, 1999-2006

Standard Notation Only Version

©2020 Roger Hudson ©2020 Roger Hudson Music
ALL RIGHTS RESERVED, INTERNATIONAL COPYRIGHT SECURED, ASCAP

No part of this publication may be reproduced in whole or in part, or stored in a retrieval system, or transmitted in any form or by any means, electronic, mechanical, photocopy, or otherwise, without written permission of the author/publisher

Cover Art by Elijah Hudson
Back cover photo by Donna Jones Bailey
www.rogerhudson.com

Preface and Timeline

This collection is a reflection of my changing life after moving to Nashville in 1997. I apparently composed many pieces in 1999! This is a fact that I did not know until I started compiling these collections! Volume 1 spans the years 1988 – 1999. I found that since so many pieces were dated 1999, I decided to start with 1999 for this collection – Volume 2. Volume 2 also contains roughly the same amount of music but within a shorter time frame – 1999-2006. After performing for Chet Atkins in Georgia, I forged professional and personal relationships with many people associated with Chet. One of the first people who showed an interest in my work was William Piburn. Bill is a prolific arranger and a fine guitarist. He was also the editor of *Fingerstyle Guitar Magazine* from 2001-2010. Bill asked me to start writing a series called "Fingerstyle Basics". The task set before me was to compose simple original pieces addressing certain techniques. These pieces needed to be one or maybe two pages long. He also wanted them to be typeset, recorded, and with an accompanying well-written column/tutorial. Evidently, according to Bill, this is a rare skill set among guitarists! So, I did all that myself for over 20 issues in *Fingerstyle Guitar*. Bill continues to regularly ask me to contribute to his current webzine called *Fingerstyle Guitar Journal*. Many of the early "Fingerstyle Basics" one-page pieces are included in this collection. The relationship with Piburn has proved as a catalyst for writing simpler, shorter forms – perfect for students. A little before this time, my children were very young and I spent many an evening trying to get them settled for bed. I also needed to release some new music. The perfect solution was to compose lullabies *while* putting them to sleep! Most of the pieces on my 2004 *Guitar Peace* album are lullabies.

Upon deciding to move to Nashville, my intention was to embark on a new career that included less teaching and more performing and recording in multiple genres. However, I was not in Nashville long before I was known as a "classical" guitar player – probably my own doing. In Nashville, that label could be a badge of honor or ridicule depending upon the source. I was a little confused and annoyed with being lumped into a category of guitarists who stereotypically could not improvise or play by ear – considering I played by ear before learning to read music. After William Yelverton's commissioning and Nashville premiere of my first guitar concerto, *Cumberland Concerto for Guitar and Strings,* several Nashville musicians and "suits" would ask me, "who orchestrated it?"! My response was always a puzzled "well…I did". Oh well, I guess I was "classical" after all…

A couple of Nashville area classical musicians that appreciated my composing, playing and teaching were Dr. Stanley Yates and Dr. William Yelverton. Both were excellent classical guitarists and headed programs at their respective schools (Austin Peay State University and Middle Tennessee State University). Both asked me to assist them as an adjunct instructor. Alas, I was teaching again. As much as I did not really set out to do more teaching, I was happy to be asked and thankful that I could. Early on in my relationship with Dr. Yates, I realized that he had a passion for new music and performing it. So, it was for Yates that I originally composed "Delta" as part of a "Blues Suite". All three of the pieces in the suite are included in this collection: Mystery, Walking, and Delta. Yates was the first concert guitarist to ever premiere one of my works. In fact, at the time, I did not even play "Delta" myself – much less the entire suite. That all changed after Yates returned from a U.K. tour, performing "Delta" as a finale. Stanley enthusiastically told me that he typically got a standing ovation with that piece and that I, "had better start playing it!". The version that I originally gave to Yates in '99 was published with his fingerings. The version here contains my fingerings and is based on my 2009 *Delta* recording – i.e. after I had started playing it! "Delta" has gone on to be one my most performed – and most difficult - pieces.

As was the case in Volume 1, I did make some updates (and corrections) to the original versions. "Indigo" and "Sorry Charlie" are two pieces that I welcome advanced players to tackle, as I have not even performed them myself!

Roger Hudson - March 2020

Roger Hudson

Solo Guitar Works Volume 2,
1999-2006

Table of Contents

Ancestral Bells..4
Asian Lullaby..5
At Sunset...6
Blue Sky...7
Bossa Nostalgia..8
Castle Lullaby..12
Close Your Eyes...14
Cool Colors..16
Cuna de Navidad...17
Delta..20
Elegy for a Surfer...26
Etude for Pinky..28
Fandango...29
Goodnight Prince...30
Harp Strings..32
Homecoming...34
Indigo..40
Interlude...51
Mystery...52
Night Ride..56
Rainy Reprise..58
Rainy Scene..60
Riffs..62
Sambuvacation..69
Siesta Impromptu..70
Sorry Charlie...71
Walking...74
Waterlily...78

©2020 Roger Hudson Music
All Rights Reserved. International copyright reserved. ASCAP
www.rogerhudson.com

Ancestral Bells

Capo on III

Relaxed, not rushed

Roger Hudson

©2003 Roger Hudson. ©2020 Roger Hudson Music. All rights reserved. International Copyright Secured. ASCAP

Asian Lullaby

Roger Hudson

Slowly and Gracefully

At Sunset

Roger Hudson

Blue Sky

Bossa Nostalgia

Roger Hudson

Castle Lullaby

Roger Hudson

Intentional blank page to minimize page turns

Close Your Eyes

(Lullaby)

Roger Hudson

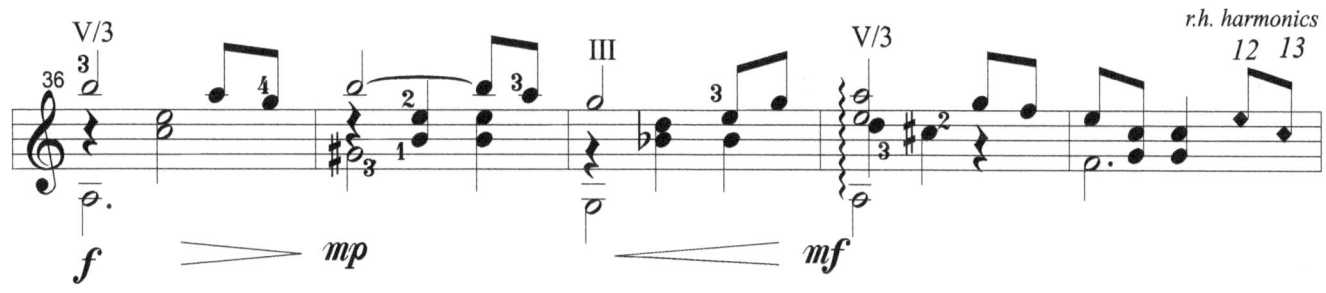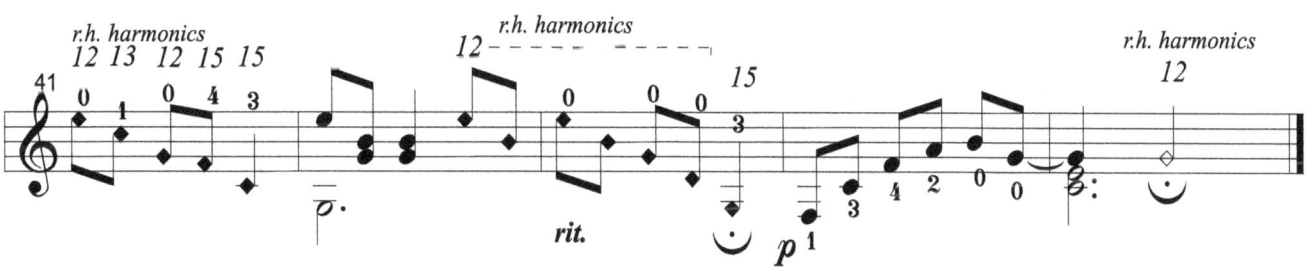

Cool Colors

Roger Hudson

©2006 Roger Hudson ©2020 Roger Hudson Music. All Rights Reserved. International Copyright Secured (ASCAP)

Cuna de Navidad
Christmas Cradle Song

Roger Hudson

Delta

from "Blues Suite"

♩. 𝅗𝅥 = 62

Roger Hudson

Espressivo con un poco "Twang"

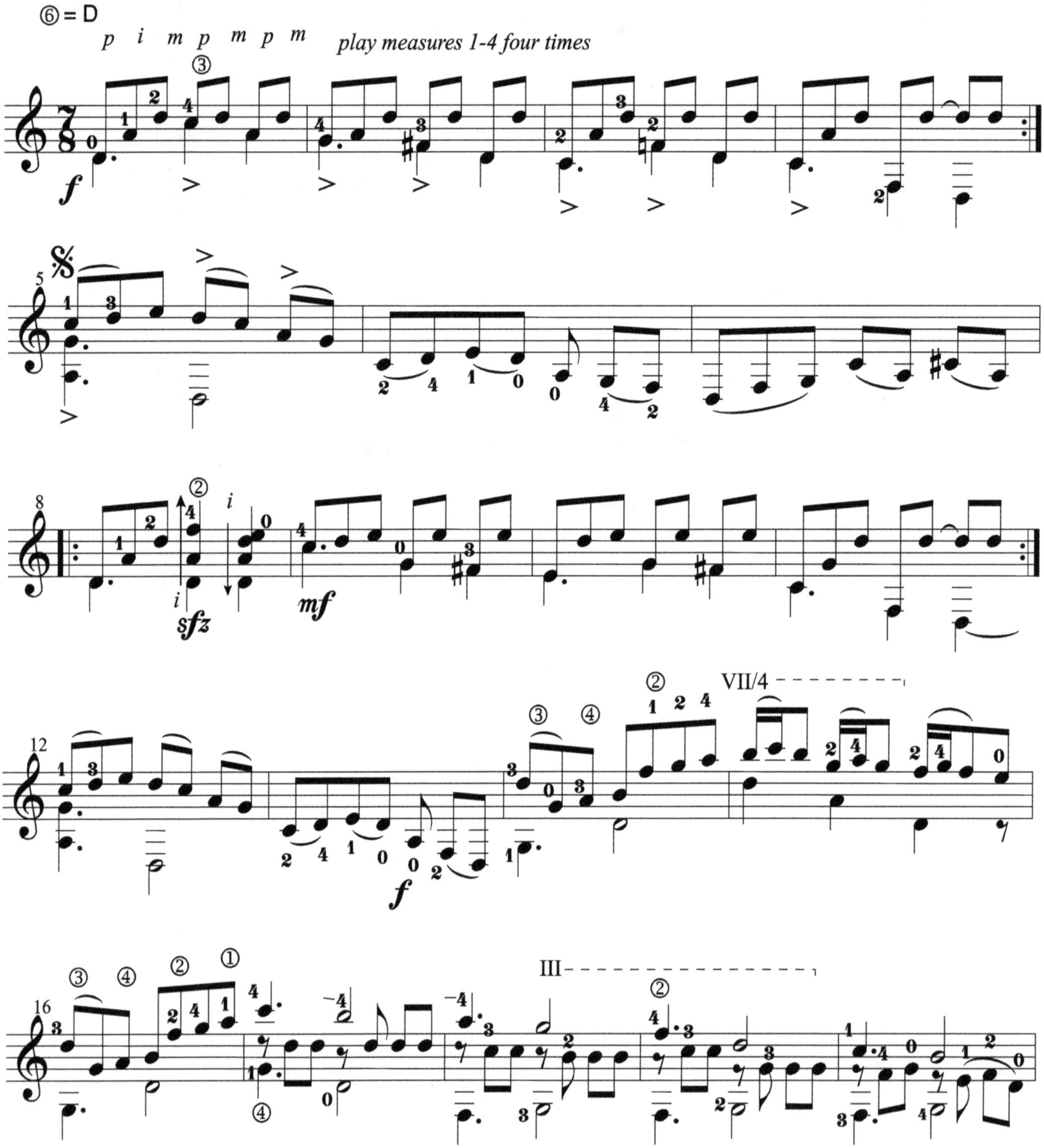
⑥ = D
p i m p m p m
play measures 1-4 four times
VII/4
III

Elegy for a Surfer
in memory of Michael

Roger Hudson

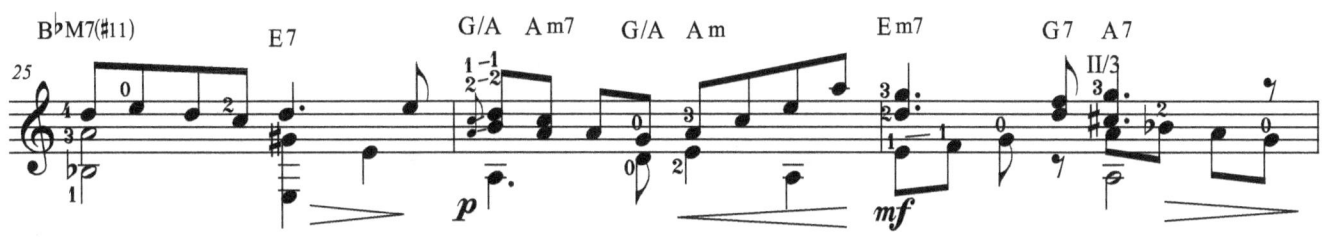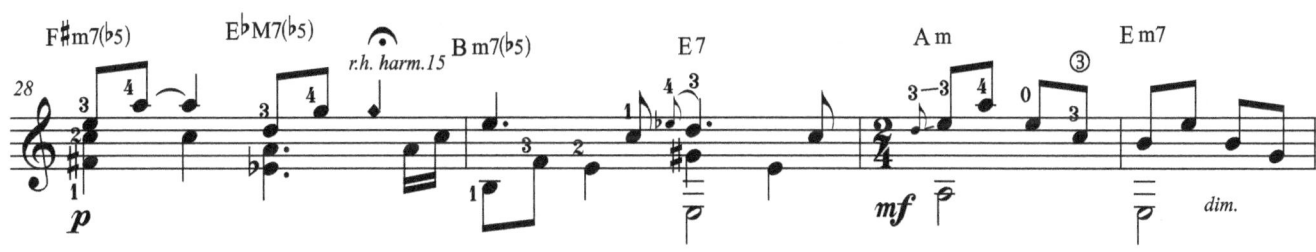

Etude for Pinky

Roger Hudson

Fandango

Roger Hudson

Goodnight Prince
(Lullaby for Elijah)

Roger Hudson

Intentional blank page to minimize page turns

Harp Strings

Roger Hudson

©2003 Roger Hudson ©2020 Roger Hudson Music. All rights reserved. International copyright secured. ASCAP

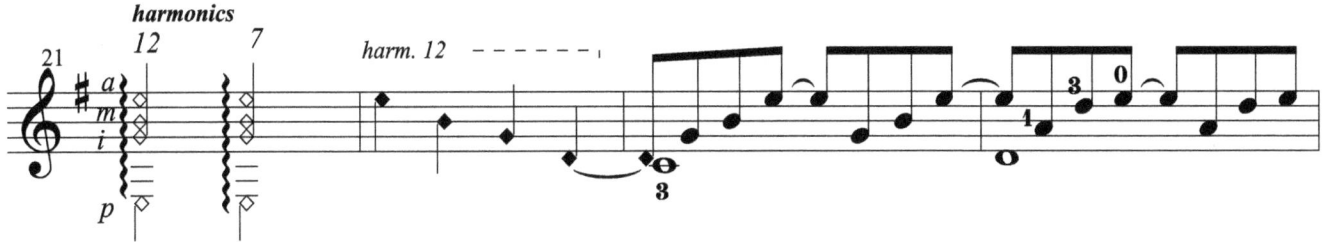
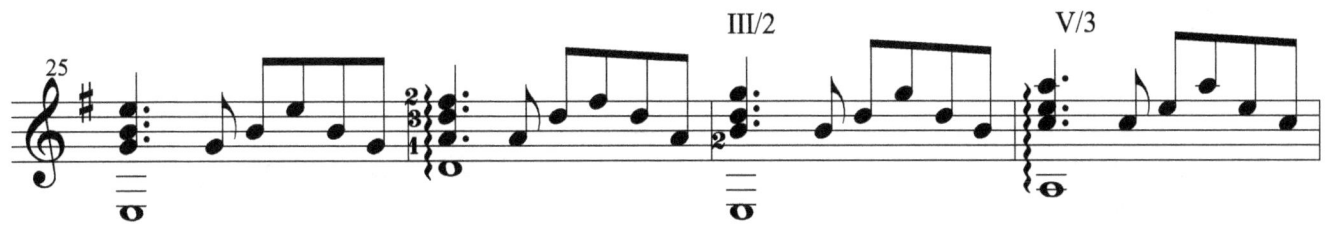
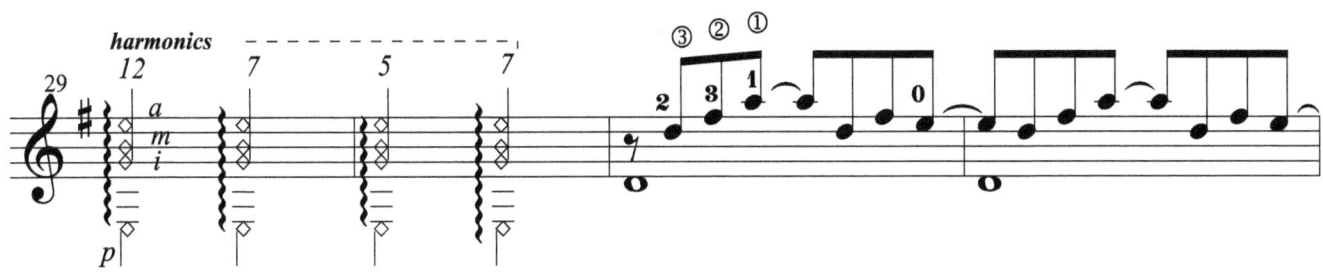

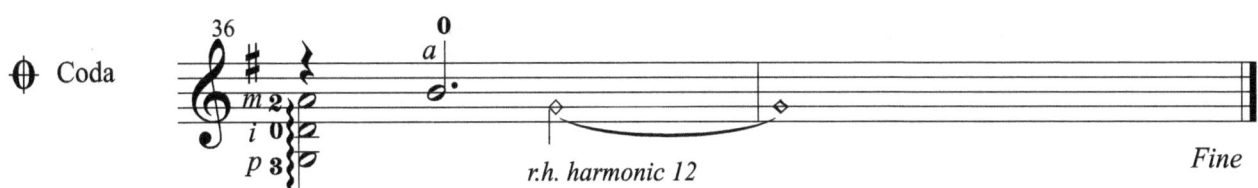

Homecoming

Capo on II

Roger Hudson

Gentle Dance

Intentional blank page to minimize page turns

Indigo

Roger Hudson

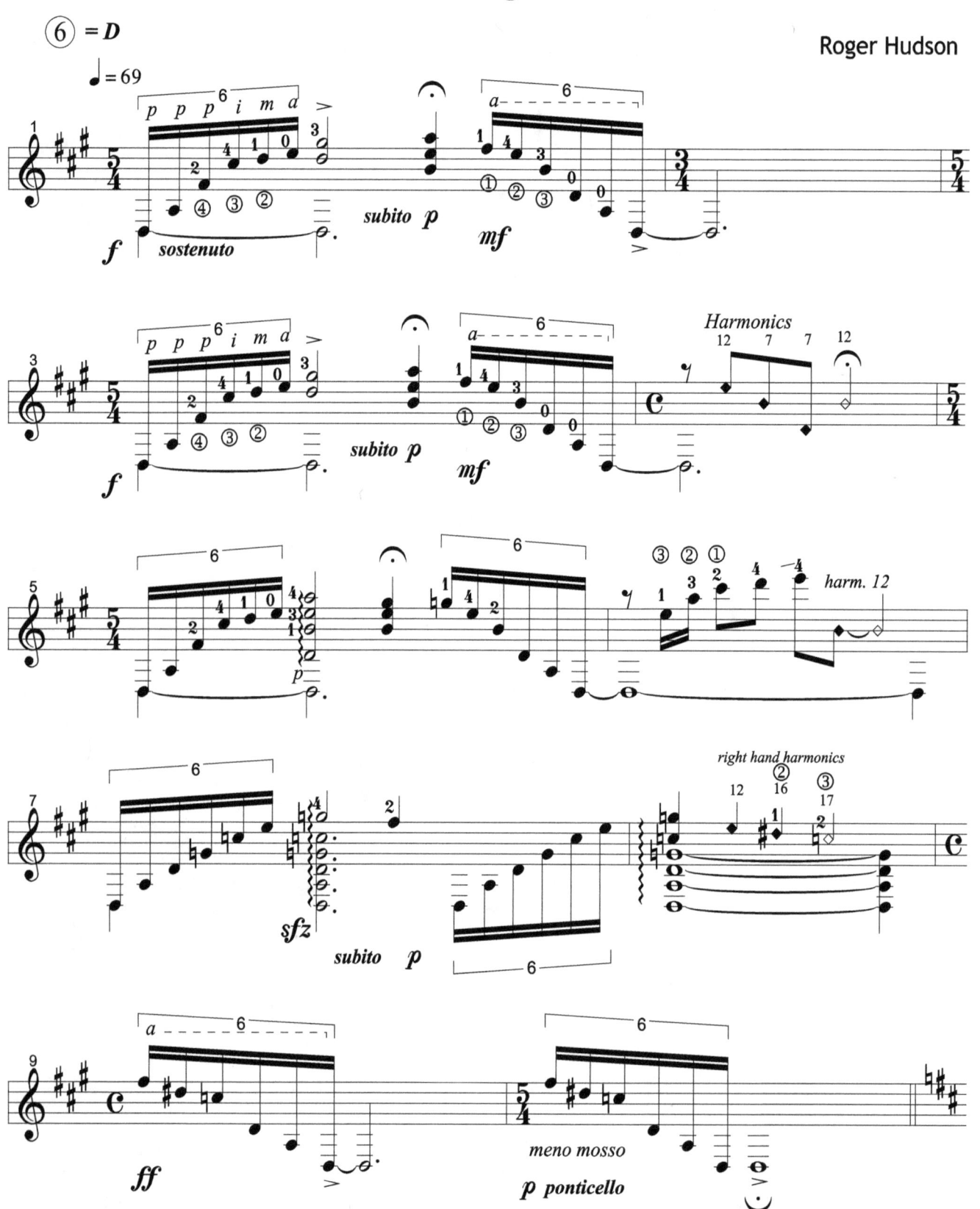

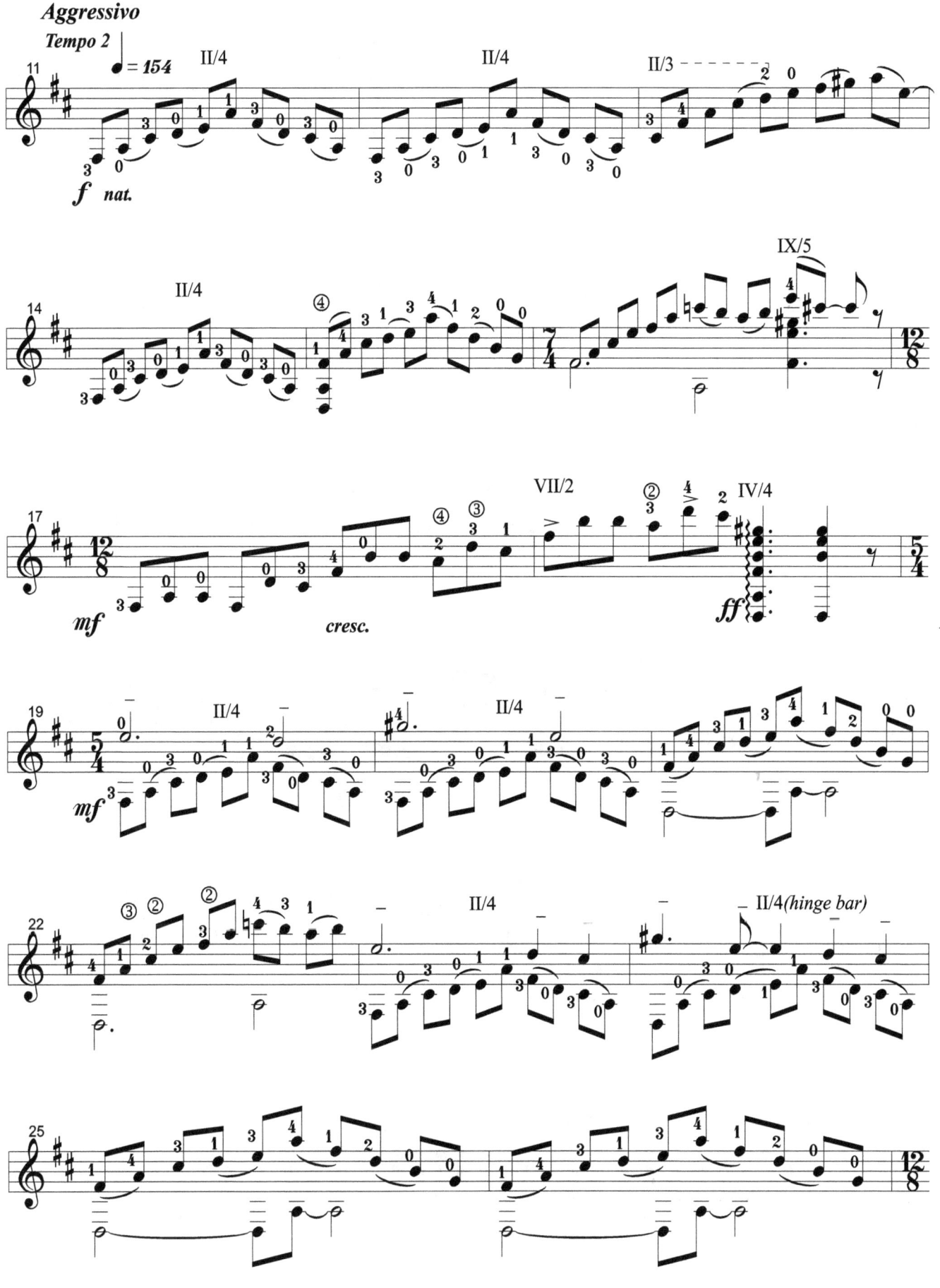

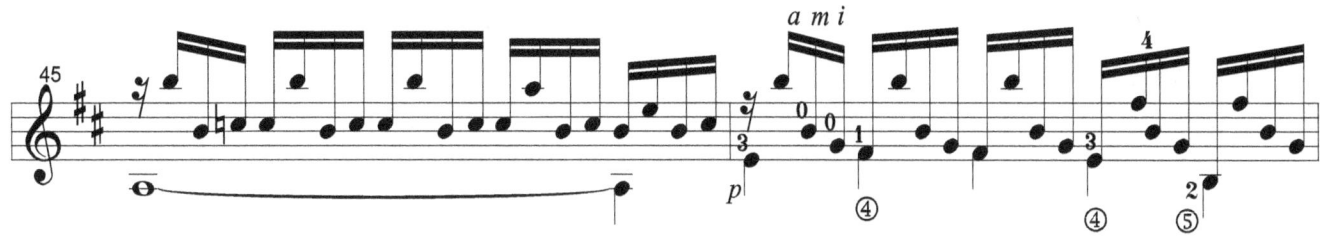
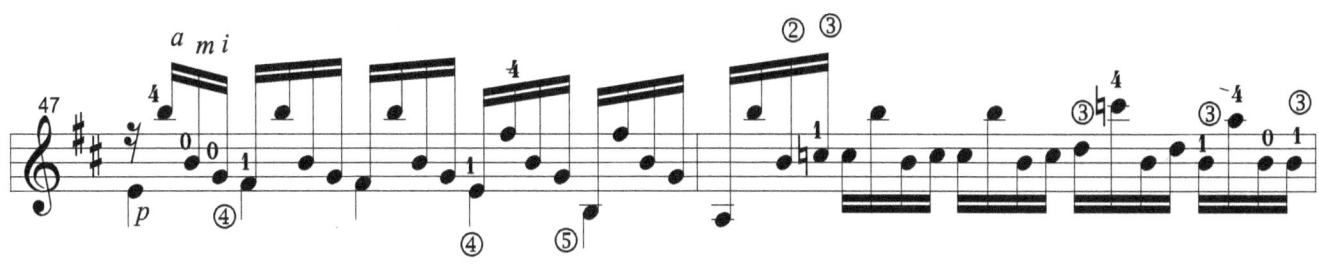
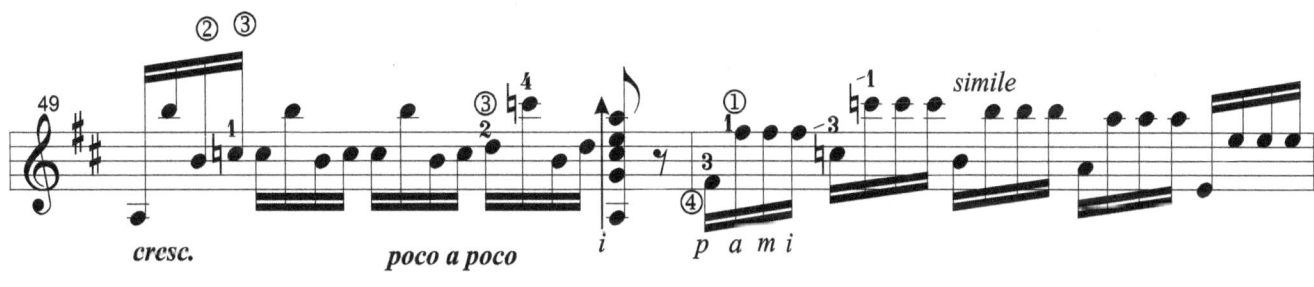
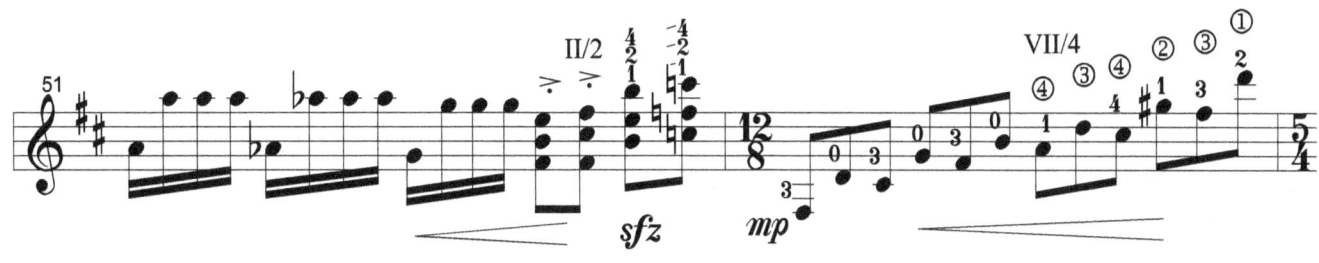

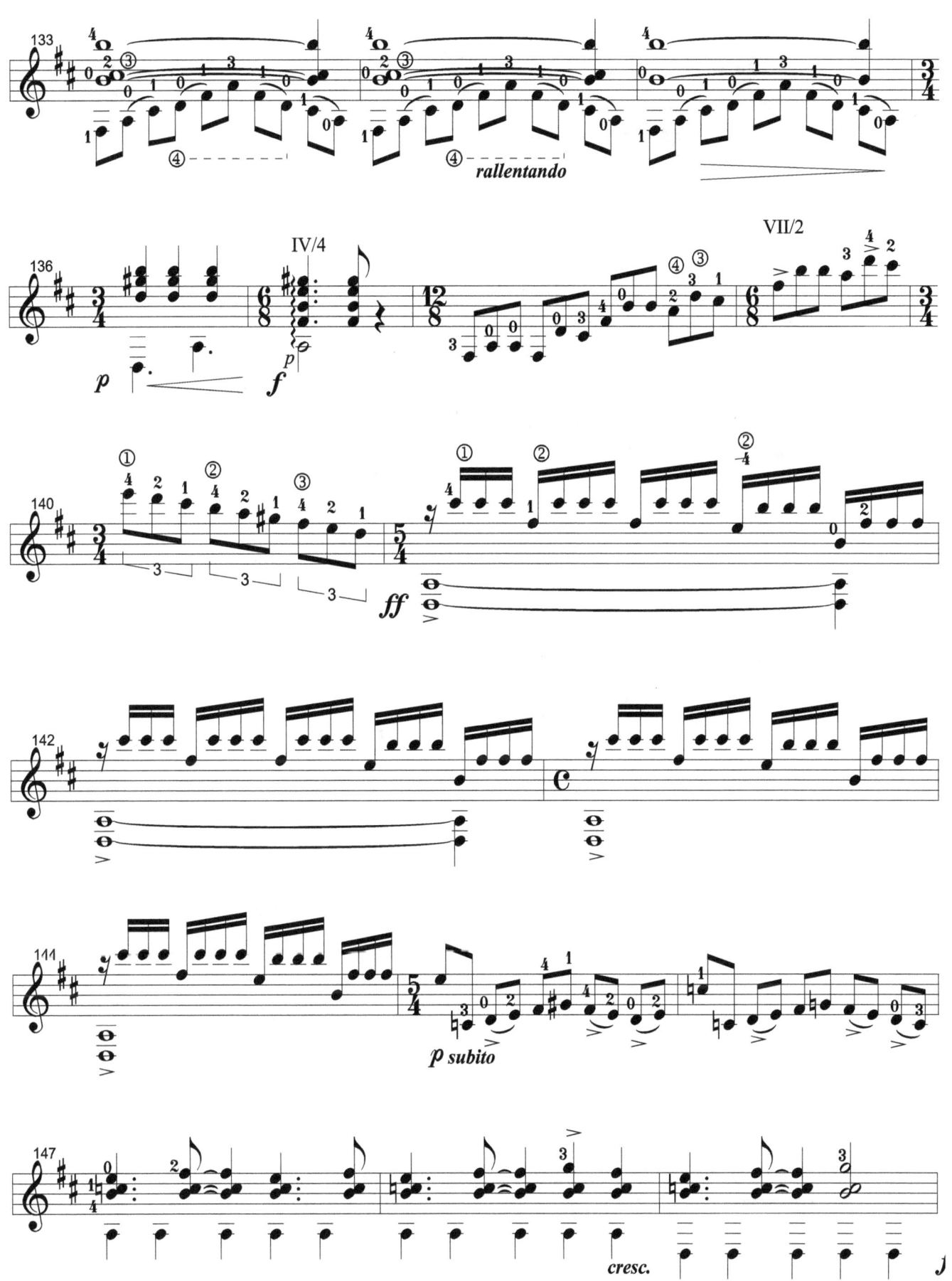

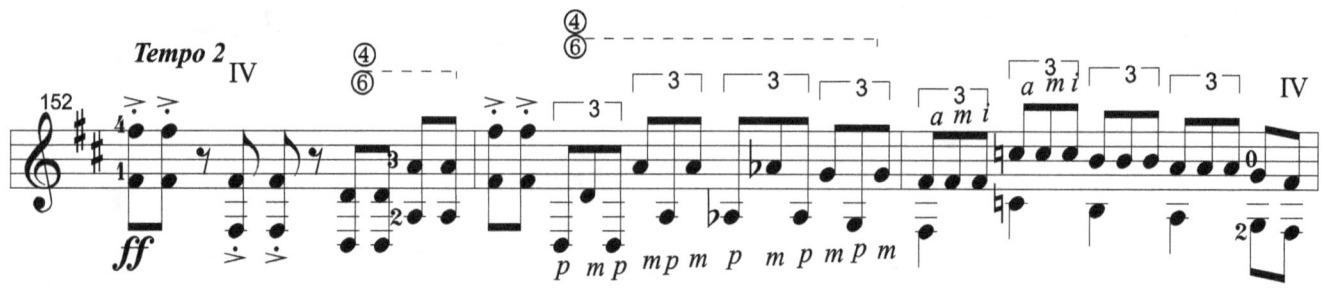

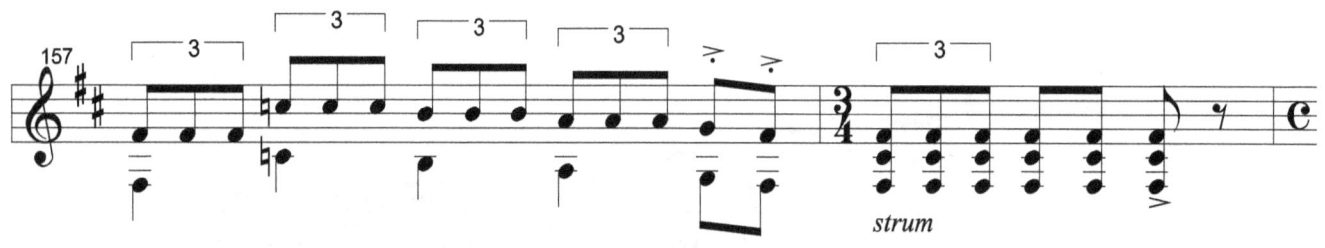
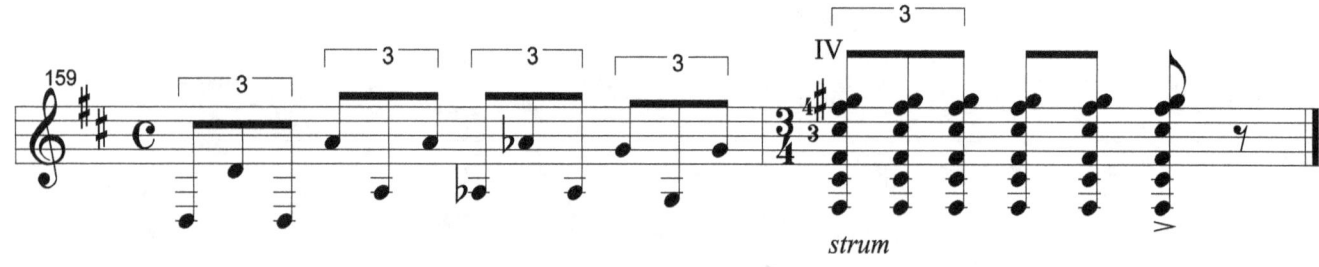

Interlude
Study in 3rds, 6ths and 10ths

Roger Hudson

Mystery
from "Blues Suite"

Roger Hudson

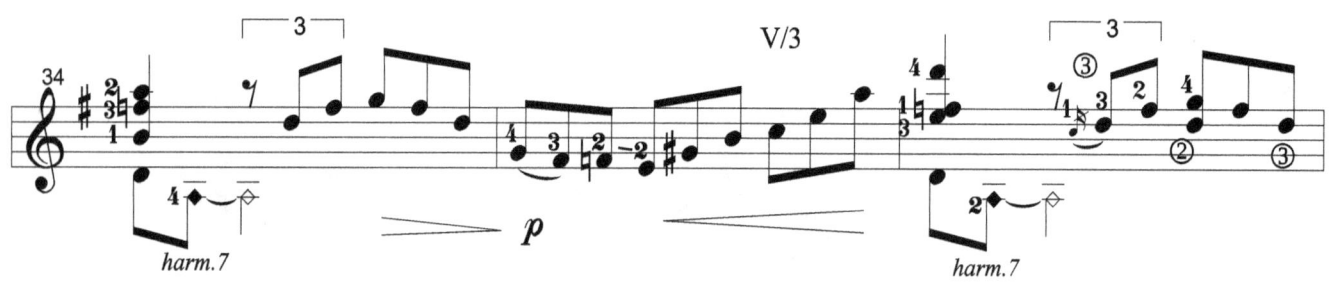

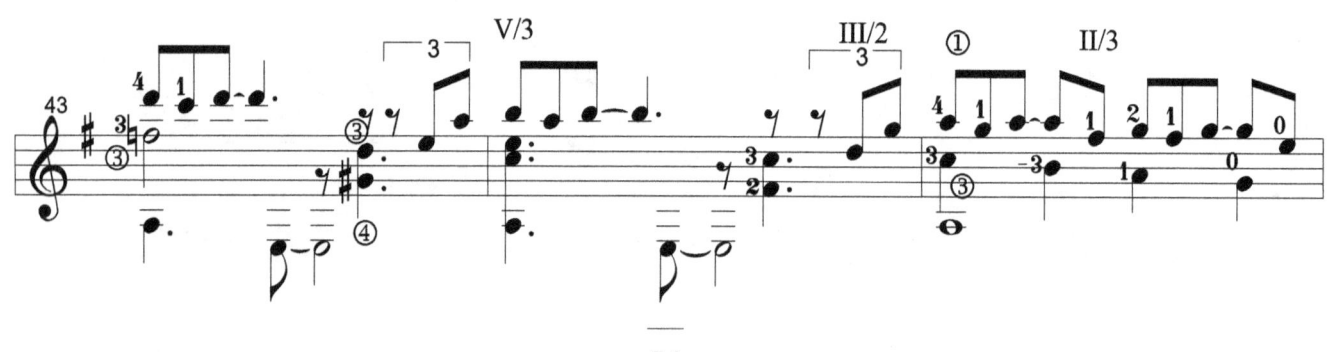

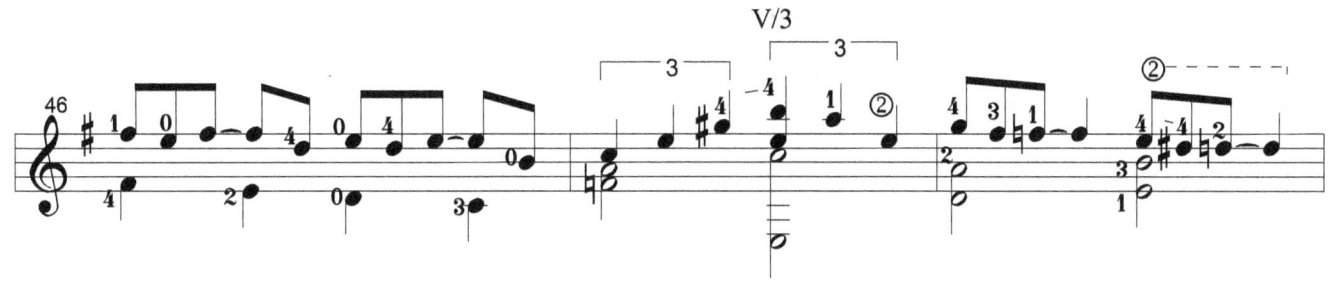

rit.   *a tempo*

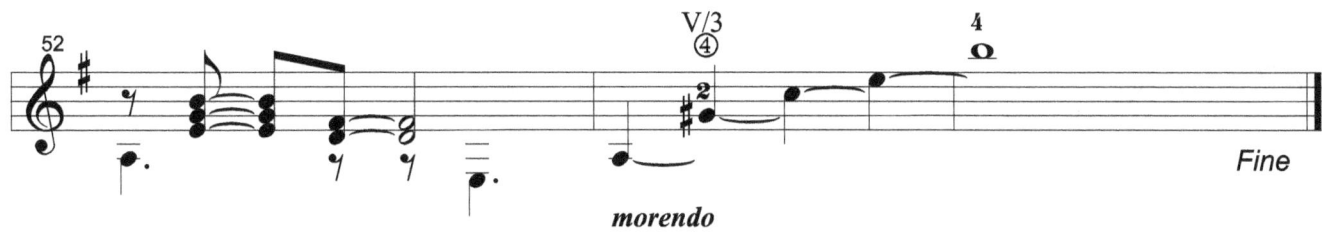

morendo   *Fine*

Night Ride

Roger Hudson

Intentional blank page to minimize page turns

Rainy Reprise

Roger Hudson

Rainy Scene

Reflectively Roger Hudson

61

Riffs

Roger Hudson

Sambavacation

Roger Hudson

Siesta Impromptu

Roger Hudson

Sorry Charlie

Roger Hudson

Ragtime Feel

Walking
from "Blues Suite"

Roger Hudson

Waterlily

Roger Hudson

©2001 Roger Hudson ©2020 Roger Hudson Music. All rights reserved. International Copyright secured (ASCAP)

www.ingramcontent.com/pod-product-compliance
Lightning Source LLC
Chambersburg PA
CBHW080601090426
42735CB00016B/3313